Geordie Sinatra

A Play

Fiona Evans

Samuel French
www.samuelfrench-london.co.uk
www.samuelfrench.com (US)

Copyright ©, (Acting Edition), BY FIONA EVANS 2013

Rights of Performance by Amateurs are controlled by Samuel French Ltd, 52 Fitzroy Street, London W1T 5JR, and they, or their authorized agents, issue licences to amateurs on payment of a fee. **It is an infringement of the Copyright to give any performance or public reading of the play before the fee has been paid and the licence issued.**
The Royalty Fee indicated below is subject to contract and subject to variation at the sole discretion of Samuel French Ltd.

> Basic fee for each and every
> performance by amateurs   Code L
> in the British Isles

The Professional Rights in this play are controlled by United Agents LLP, 12-26 Lexington Street, London W1F 0LE. www.unitedagents.co.uk

---

The publication of this play does not imply that it is necessarily available for performance by amateurs or professionals, either in the British Isles or Overseas. Amateurs and professionals considering a production are strongly advised in their own interests to apply to the appropriate agents for written consent before starting rehearsals or booking a theatre or hall.

ISBN 978 0 573 11185 3

The right of Fiona Evans to be identified as author
of this work has been asserted in accordance with
Section 77 of the Copyright, Designs and Patents Act 1988

First published in 2012 by New Writing North

Please see page iv for further copyright information

GEORDIE SINATRA

First performed at Live Theatre, Newcastle upon Tyne, on 18 April to 12 May and then at the Stephen Joseph Theatre, Scarborough, from 16 May to 2 June 2012, with the following cast:

Geordie/Frank Sinatra*	Anthony Cable
Officer/Sonny/Jimmy Van Heusen*	Kraig Thornber
Joan/Dolly Sinatra*	Jill Myers
Nancy/Ava Gardner*/Vera	Heather Saunders
Pianist/Bill Miller*/Vicar	Richard Atkinson

Director	Chris Monks
Designer	Jan Bee Brown
Musical Director	Richard Atkinson
Lighting Director	Mark Johnson
Sound Designer	Martin Hodgson
Choreographer	Bev Edmunds
Wardrobe Supervisor	Lou Duffy

* *These characters form part of Geordie's hallucinations. They are not meant to be an accurate representation of any person living or dead.*

COPYRIGHT INFORMATION

(See also page ii)

This play is fully protected under the Copyright Laws of the British Commonwealth of Nations, the United States of America and all countries of the Berne and Universal Copyright Conventions.

All rights including Stage, Motion Picture, Radio, Television, Public Reading, and Translation into Foreign Languages, are strictly reserved.

No part of this publication may lawfully be reproduced in ANY form or by any means — photocopying, typescript, recording (including video-recording), manuscript, electronic, mechanical, or otherwise — or be transmitted or stored in a retrieval system, without prior permission.

Licences for amateur performances are issued subject to the understanding that it shall be made clear in all advertising matter that the audience will witness an amateur performance; that the names of the authors of the plays shall be included on all programmes; and that the integrity of the authors' work will be preserved.

The Royalty Fee is subject to contract and subject to variation at the sole discretion of Samuel French Ltd.

In Theatres or Halls seating Four Hundred or more the fee will be subject to negotiation.

In Territories Overseas the fee quoted above may not apply. A fee will be quoted on application to our local authorized agent, or if there is no such agent, on application to Samuel French Ltd, London.

VIDEO-RECORDING OF AMATEUR PRODUCTIONS

Please note that the copyright laws governing video-recording are extremely complex and that it should not be assumed that any play may be video-recorded for whatever purpose without first obtaining the permission of the appropriate agents. The fact that a play is published by Samuel French Ltd does not indicate that video rights are available or that Samuel French Ltd controls such rights.

CHARACTERS

Geordie/Frank Sinatra, 70ish male
Nancy/Ava Gardner/Vera, 40ish female
Joan/Dolly Sinatra, 60ish female
Officer/Sonny/Jimmy Van Heusen, 60ish male
Pianist/Bill Miller/Vicar, male

COPYRIGHT MUSIC

A licence issued by Samuel French Ltd to perform this play does not include permission to use any Incidental music specified in this copy. Where the place of performance is already licensed by the PERFORMING RIGHT SOCIETY a return of the music used must be made to them. If the place of performance is not so licensed then application should be made to the Performing Right Society, 29 Berners Street, London Wl.

A separate and additional licence from PHONOGRAPHIC PERFORMANCES LTD, 1 Upper James Street, London W1R 3HG is needed whenever commercial recordings are used.

The Lewy Body Society, established in June 2006 in the UK, is the only charity in Europe exclusively concerned with dementia with Lewy bodies. The charity's mission is to raise awareness of DLB for the general public and educate those in the medical profession and decision-making positions about all aspects of the disease and to support research into the disease. For more information, see www.lewbody.org.

Alzheimer's Society is a membership organisation which works to improve the quality of life of people affected by dementia in England, Wales and Northern Ireland. For more information about their work, go to www.alzheimers.org.uk.

FOREWORD

My wonderful dad David 'Geordie' Evans was diagnosed with vascular dementia in 2009.

To help deal with this, I started reading about the disease and came across a condition, dementia with Lewy bodies (DLB), where people hallucinate. Dad didn't have DLB, but he experienced hallucinations, usually small animals, but on occasions people, including his sister Kathleen — who died in 1946! Although this was a worry, as a dramatist, it sparked my interest and *Geordie Sinatra* was conceived.

The play had to have music — it is one of the few pleasures that someone with advanced dementia can enjoy. Song lyrics will often be remembered when a person can't even recognise their own children. Why Frank? Sinatra's personal life was every bit as interesting as his career. As Bono put it, "To sing like that you've gotta have lost a couple of fights ... you've gotta have had your heart broken." Frank's voice is a manifestation of his life experiences, it commands dignity and respect, and a person with dementia should be viewed and appreciated in much the same way. Humour was also a vital ingredient, as families coping with dementia often laugh together, rather than cry.

Geordie Sinatra is not autobiographical, but at the heart of it is a strong father/daughter relationship. My dad's illness reversed the roles in our relationship. He had always cared for me. Now I had to grow up and take some responsibility. Dementia may have taken away with one hand, but it has given me something else with the other. It's brought our family together, given me a new appreciation of my parents, made me value the small things in life — talking to someone, listening, smiling and making them feel valued.

Dementia has forced me to reassess my own priorities and taught me to live life in the present. Hopefully, *Geordie Sinatra* contributes in some small way to raising awareness of dementia and gets us thinking about how we should care.

I would like to thank ... SJT artistic director Chris Monks, and Max Roberts, Artistic Director at Live Theatre, for commissioning the play. Gez Casey, Literary Manager at Live Theatre, and Chris for invaluable script development. Kate Rowland for being a well-timed outside eye. New Writing North for initiating the whole project. Our partners at Newcastle Science City, ERDF, Changing Age and the Alzheimer's Society, especially those at the Connie Lewcock Centre. Professor Ian McKeith and Peter Ashley (Lewy Body Society) for giving me a unique insight into DLB. The Maudsley Charity for their support. My fellow writers Romi Jones, Rebecca Jenkins and Valerie Laws. Special thanks is reserved for Steve Cooper, comedy writing partner and Frank to my Ava — plenty of arguing but no sex! Without Steve's friendship, support and major contribution, *Geordie Sinatra* would not exist. I owe you, kid. And, of course, my wonderful family.

Fiona Evans

PRODUCTION NOTE

In the original production the cast members formed part of the band (during Geordie's hallucinations) to accompany the pianist. At the end of the play, during the final gig, they played instruments as their characters — the Vicar/Officer/Joan/Nancy.

At the beginning of Act II in the duel with the headlines, these were originally written on big cards which the actors danced around with. This may be left to the director or designer's interpretation.

Fiona Evans

This play is dedicated to David 'Geordie' Evans,
the best dad in the world

ACT I

Prologue

Sands Hotel cabaret bar, Vegas/Morrisons, Whitley Bay

Geordie is hallucinating

Compère (*recorded speech*) Welcome, ladies and gentlemen, to the Sands Hotel, Las Vegas; the coolest most happening joint in town. Kick back, snap a Dunhill and grab yourself a whiskey sour. Let "The Chairman of the Board" transport you to paradise. I give you "The Voice", Mr Francis Albert Sinatra...

Canned applause and cheers

Geordie appears as Frank Sinatra, dressed in a tuxedo, and sings a snatch of the Frank Sinatra song "Come Fly With Me"

Geordie How did all these folk get in my room?

Canned laughter and clapping, Geordie takes a bow. Cameras flash

What the hell...?

Harsh lights up to reveal a confused Geordie standing with skewiff toupée, trousers round ankles and a shopping basket in his hand

Recorded supermarket tannoy announcement: "Security to aisle five."

Black-out

Scene 1

Sands Hotel cabaret bar, Whitley Bay

The scruffy cabaret cellar bar of the Sands Hotel, a run-down joint that hasn't seen a reveller or lick of paint in years. A home-made poster is pinned up: Geordie Sinatra, Comeback Gig. Various photos of musicians hang on the wall, including ones of young Geordie, Vera and Sonny. Joan is sitting at the bar, which is stocked with various bottles and glasses, and surrounded by business text books and paperwork. She's on the phone to the bank manager. Other books are stacked around the set: biographies — Frank Sinatra, Ava Gardner and other musicians — misery memoirs, etc. There is a drum kit covered with a dust sheet and a CD player

Joan Yes, I appreciate that it's a large amount, but... (*not happy with what she's hearing on the other end of the phone*) I need that money, if I'm going to... I don't have other options... Like what?... (*She looks around the place, considering*) No, that's out of the question... I can't...

Offstage sound of scuffling

I'm really sorry, I'm going to have to call you back. (*She ends the call and quickly tidies away the paperwork*)

A Police Community Support Officer and Geordie enter and come down the stairs. Geordie is struggling to free himself from the Officer, who is guiding him in. He is still wearing his tux — minus the trousers

Geordie Get your greasy mitts off my threads, you Keystone clown!
Officer Don't get abusive again, sir.
Joan Geordie! What the ——
Geordie Do you know who I am?
Officer Aye, your name and address is sewn into your jacket.
Geordie I've got friends in high places.
Officer I don't care if you know Ant and Dec, you can't dance around Morrisons with nee pants on.
Geordie Ma, tell this bum to take his fat paws offa me.
Joan Sorry, Officer.
Officer Ma? You can't be his ——
Joan No! What happened to his trousers?
Officer Very good question.
Geordie Filthy coppers! Always breaking up the party.
Joan Frank!
Officer Frank? On the label it says George Carson.
Joan We call him Frank. It's like a nickname.

The Officer eyes the posters and photos

That was him, back in the day.
Officer Geordie Sinatra, eh? Do you think you should be encouraging him?

Act I, Scene 1   3

Geordie Go to hell, Buster.
Joan Now Francis, be a good boy and keep it zipped. What happened?
Officer From what I can gather, he was belting out Sinatra tunes next to the loo rolls. Some kids started taking pictures and he—erm—exposed himself.
Joan No!
Geordie It's not what it looks like, Ma. I was only trying to teach those reporters a lesson.
Officer What in, human biology?

Geordie takes a handful of tickets from his jacket pocket and starts stuffing them in the Officer's pockets

Geordie Here, take some tickets. Gold dust. Big comeback show, next Saturday — bring a pal — bring them both.
Joan Why don't you have a little sit down while I sort this out.

Joan settles Geordie into a chair. During the rest of the scene Geordie zones out, appearing absent

Don't you worry, Dolly's got it all under control. (*To Officer*) OK flatfoot, lay it on the line. I mean — sorry Officer, what happened?
Officer Well, Dolly —
Joan Erm, no, I'm Joan. Joan Wilson.
Officer Then who's Dolly?
Joan Dolly Sinatra. Frank's mum.
Officer Right.
Joan It makes life easier.
Officer Not for me it doesn't. Who exactly are you?
Joan His wife, well, girlfriend—partner—chief cook and bottle washer.
Officer According to the witnesses... (*Reading deadpan from his notebook*) "He flipped, told us to leave him and Ava alone. He tried to grab my mobile phone, but I held on tight, so the loony dropped his trousers and said, 'Get a picture of this you fucking assholes!' "
Joan So strictly speaking it wasn't Geordie was it? It was Frank.
Officer Yes—well—no. I can hardly go back to the station saying I've arrested Frank Sinatra. They'd lock me up. Shouldn't he be in a home or summat?
Joan This is his home.
Officer (*looking at the surroundings; doubtfully*) Mmm. You're going to have to keep him inside.
Joan This isn't a prison.

Officer That's where he'll end up if he runs around in his undercrackers. (*Pause*) I'll overlook the incident this time.
Joan What about the supermarket? The kids?
Officer Supermarket don't want the adverse publicity. The kids won't complain, they got what they wanted. He's probably an internet sensation by now. (*Looking around*) Like a time capsule in here isn't it?
Joan It was the place to be, back in the day.
Officer Oh aye— "The Sands Hotel and Cabaret Bar", me Mam used to come here. Is it still a hotel?
Joan No, not for years.
Officer Shame. Waste of a good building.
Joan Yeah well—thanks for bringing him home.

Joan tries to usher the Officer out

Officer Is, er—your daughter not about?
Joan My daughter?
Officer Nancy.
Joan She's not my daughter.
Officer Oh, right, I just assumed ——
Joan You know her?
Officer She's famous, isn't she. It said in the paper she was coming back to look after her sick dad. (*Remembering the headline*) "Disgraced Gossip Queen in Mercy Dash." Geordie's label. Same last name. Two plus two. Police training.
Joan We can all sleep easy.
Officer Miscarriage of justice if you ask me. Nancy getting the big E from the *Daily Mail*. Is her husband really as crooked as they make out?
Joan No comment.
Officer "Playboy bookie in nag-nobbling *ménage à trois*". That's what it said, in her own paper!
Joan I preferred the *Star*'s 'Wag-Shag-Nag-Bag'. Still, if you dish it out...
Officer Poor Nancy. Did they really freeze all her assets?
Joan She's Audi-less. Why do you think she's here?
Officer To care for the old man.
Joan Oh yeah, regular Mother Teresa is our Nancy.

Nancy enters, carrying a bag, mobile phone to her ear

It's your lucky day, it's the scribbling nun herself.
Nancy (*on the phone, totally self-absorbed*) A romance novel? You must be fucking joking! Have you any idea what I'm going through?...

Act I, Scene 1 5

    You try reinventing yourself when you've got to wipe your father's backside...

Joan looks annoyed at the lie

    No Julian, I don't want to write about dementia, it's depressing... Zeitgeisty? Is it?... Listen darling, I'm exhausted, leave it with me. I might be able to find an angle. (*She ends the call, then notices the Officer*)
Officer It's an honour to meet you, Miss Carson.
Nancy Am I under arrest?
Officer Oh, no. No, no, no! (*He stares at Nancy*)
Joan He's that fan you mentioned.
Nancy How wonderful for him. Can you stop him staring?
Joan Stop staring at her.

The Officer is in a trance

    Hey, Inspector Clueless!
Officer Sorry. Could I have your autograph, please?
Nancy Of course you can.
Officer Well, for me mam, like.
Nancy Always happy to oblige fans.

The Officer whips out a copy of the "Daily Mail" with the "Nag-Nobbling" headline emblazoned and gives it to Nancy; she isn't impressed

    Who should I make it out to...?
Officer Chris.
Joan That's your name isn't it?
Officer How do you know?
Joan Says on your notebook.
Officer Oh, aye. Me mam's called Chris too, Christine.
Nancy So, to Christine?
Officer (*wanting it for himself*) No, just put Chris.

Nancy puts her bag down, takes a pen out of it, and signs the paper but holds onto it

    Thank you so much—I—she'll really appreciate it.
Nancy All part of the service. That'll be a tenner.
Officer I thought——
Nancy It's not personal, Officer, it's business. I wouldn't expect you to beat up a suspect without getting paid for it.

Joan Oh, just give him it, he brought your dad back.
Nancy (*concerned*) Where from?
Joan "Frank" made a personal appearance. In Morrisons.
Nancy He shouldn't be wandering the streets.

The Officer goes to hand Nancy a tenner

Just have it. Did anybody see him?
Joan Ashamed?
Nancy No! I'm concerned. What happened to his trousers?
Joan Lost them in toiletries.
Officer At least he's calmed down now.
Joan It comes in waves. One moment he's perfectly lucid...
Nancy The next he's away with the chorus girls. If I didn't know better, I'd swear he's putting it on.
Joan He's not putting it on.
Nancy I wish to God he was.
Officer Is it Alzheimer's?
Joan Something similar.
Officer Me nan had Alzheimer's.
Joan It's dementia with Lewy bodies.
Officer Never heard of it.
Joan Not a lot of people have.
Officer How come he thinks he's Frank Sinatra?
Joan One of the symptoms is hallucinations.
Officer He sees things?
Joan And hears stuff.
Officer Like what?
Nancy Ava Gardner.
Officer Who's she?
Nancy Who cares?
Joan Frank Sinatra's second wife and Hollywood star. (*She selects a book and hands it to the Officer*) They said she was the most beautiful woman in the world.
Officer I wouldn't mind hallucinating about her.
Joan It's not all Hollywood glamour, some of his visions can be really disturbing.
Officer Poor Geordie.
Nancy Poor Geordie? What about poor Nancy? It's me that's got to deal with this, he's as happy as a sandboy.
Joan Real saint, isn't she?
Nancy Actually officer, seeing as you're a fan. I was wondering if I could run something by you? Something I'm working on.

Act I, Scene 1

Officer I'd be honoured.
Nancy A book. My debut novel.
Sonny Brilliant idea.
Nancy My heroine. I'm thinking of making her a carer for an elderly relative.
Joan Fiction?
Nancy Romance!

Involuntary laugh from Joan

Officer I love Mills and Boon. Well, me mam does.
Nancy Obviously I'll draw on my own personal experience, but the character will be quite different from me—plain, frumpy. As a man, how would you respond to that? Is it sexy enough?
Officer Oh I like frumpy lasses—the big pant brigade does it for me.
Nancy Excellent. (*To Joan*) Dust down your Dutch cap, you might be in there.

There is a crackled message from the Officer's radio

Officer Geordie, I'm going to go now, but I need you to promise to behave yourself.
Joan It's impossible to rouse him when he's like this.
Officer You can't keep going round breaking the law. Are you listening?

The Officer waves his hand in front of Geordie's face. Geordie doesn't respond

Do you think he's OK? Might he be, you know, having one now?
Joan You never can tell.

The lights change, and we are transported into Geordie's hallucination. Geordie sings a snatch of Frank Sinatra's song "Don't Be A Do-Badder". Joan, Nancy and Sonny join in singing, and throw themselves into a dance routine

At the end of the song, the lights change back, and we move from hallucination back into reality. Everyone in their original positions

Officer Absolutely nothing going on.

Black-out

SCENE 2

The same

Nancy is speaking into a Dictaphone

Joan enters unnoticed and listens to Nancy's efforts with amusement

Nancy (*into the Dictaphone*) A tear came to Fanny's eye as Doctor Eros broke the news: her father had dementia. It was a day she would never forget. Not least because it was the day she met her husband. She was irresistibly drawn to the hunky Canadian medic's impressive jaw-line, his five o'clock shadow and the musky smell of—the musky smell of —
Joan His beaver hat?
Nancy Creeping Jesus. Can you stop doing that?
Joan Doing what?
Nancy Loitering, I'm trying to work.
Joan I do live here.
Nancy Pity.
Joan I thought dementia was "depressing".
Nancy It's not about dementia, it's about struggle, about loss, it's about —
Joan You?
Nancy No.
Joan Well, I bet it's not about your dad.
Nancy If I need your input, I'll...

Nancy's phone starts ringing. She looks at the screen to see who's ringing, and clicks it off

Joan Reporters?
Nancy (*not wanting to go there, so changing the subject to the Geordie Sinatra poster*) Did you do this?
Joan Me and Geordie.
Nancy "Comeback Gig"? He'll only get upset when he finds out it's all bullshit.
Joan It stimulates him.
Nancy It gets him over-excited.
Joan Everyone needs a bit of excitement in their lives.
Nancy Yes, well, I've had enough excitement to last a lifetime.
Joan Sorry, I... if you want to talk...
Nancy I want to work, but I keep being interrupted —

Act I, Scene 2

Sonny enters and comes down the stairs. He looks around the room taking it all in. He looks at the old photos hanging on the wall and lingers on the photo of Vera

Who the hell's this?
Joan How should I know?
Nancy Don't you ever lock that front door? People are just wandering in off the bloody street.
Joan I'd better check on —
Nancy Don't leave me with him. He could be an axe murderer... (*To Sonny*) Excuse me. This is private living quarters. (*Pause*) Oi, cloth ears!
Sonny (*broken from his reverie; with a transatlantic twang*) Sorry ladies. I'm just blown away by the old place. (*He becomes transfixed by Nancy*)
Nancy Oh, an American?
Sonny No. I was born and raised in Scarborough. I used to gig here. I'm a musician.
Nancy Oh. Not today thank you. We've got all the musicians we need.
Sonny You're Nancy.
Nancy You're creepy.
Sonny Just like your mum.
Nancy My mum?
Sonny You were so high, last time I saw you. (*He looks around*) Hasn't changed a bit. Spooky.
Joan (*stepping forward, hand outstretched*) Joan Wilson. Geordie's partner.
Sonny Sonny Gleason. Pleased to meet you, love. I don't suppose Geordie's around?
Joan } (*together*) { No. (*Beat*)Yes.
Nancy } { Yes. (*Beat*) No.
Sonny I'm confused.
Nancy Well you're in the right place.
Sonny Sorry?
Nancy Never mind. So, Sonny, you knew my mother?
Sonny Everyone knew Vera. One hell of a woman, a hard act to follow.

Joan becomes uncomfortable at the mention of Vera

Joan So I've been told. Nice to meet you, Mr Gleason.
Sonny Sonny, please.
Joan I need to get on.
Nancy Give Dad a shout while you're up there.

Joan He's probably having a nap.
Nancy Well, wake him up. You're always saying he spends too much time in bed.

Joan exits

Well, Sonny, this is quite serendipitous, you "rocking up" after all these years. You see I'm doing some research into the Sands, to help with my new novel.
Sonny Writer. Creative. It's in the blood.
Nancy Would you like a drink?
Sonny Don't mind if I do. Scotch on the rocks. Only because this is a very special occasion.

Nancy pours Sonny a drink and leaves out the bottle. As they talk, he tops himself up from time to time

Nancy, Nancy, Nancy.
Nancy Sonny, Sonny, Sonny.
Sonny My, how you have grown.
Nancy I should hope so.
Sonny I used to bounce you up and down on my knee.
Nancy Try it now and I'll stab you with my Parker. So Sonny, was Mum as beautiful as the photos?
Sonny Oh yeah. Of course, you won't remember her.
Nancy I was only three when she died.
Sonny What?
Nancy Mother died in a car crash.
Sonny A car crash?
Nancy Back in nineteen seventy-five.
Sonny (*gobsmacked*) That's terrible. I'm sorry about that.
Nancy Don't be. It's not your fault, unless you cut the brake cables? Ha!

Sonny downs his drink in one

Sonny How's Geordie?
Nancy Let's just say—things ain't what they used to be.
Sonny Eh?
Nancy He's in La-La Land.

Sonny appears unsure at what Nancy means

He's ill, dementia.

Act I, Scene 2   11

Sonny What! Geordie? No way.
Nancy I'm sure he'd be delighted to see an old friend.
Sonny If he's in a bad way... I don't think —
Nancy Don't worry it's not contagious.
Sonny Can he still remember stuff?
Nancy Some things. He gets very confused. This morning he thought I was Nancy Sinatra.
Sonny Frank's daughter?
Nancy No, Frank's wife! As if! I've seen pictures of her and she wasn't exactly a looker.
Sonny Will he remember me?
Nancy He might.
Sonny I'm sorry, this was a bad idea.
Nancy He'd love to see you, reminisce.

Joan enters with Geordie. (In his head he's Frank Sinatra)

Geordie sings the first couple of lines of Frank Sinatra's song "My Way"

Look who's here, Dad.

Geordie squints at Sonny trying to work out who he is

Sonny (*nervously*) Geordie.

Sonny and Geordie eye each other, Sonny looking for a flicker of recognition

Geordie Mr Sinatra to you.
Nancy He's gone again.
Sonny He doesn't recognize me.
Geordie Sure. Course I do.
Sonny You do?
Geordie Jimmy Van Heusen.
Nancy It's Sonny.
Geordie Sonny?
Sonny Sonny Gleason, your old sidekick.
Geordie You goddamn son-of-a-bitch. Good to see you pal.

Geordie embraces Sonny. Sonny is relieved

I thought for a minute you were Van Heusen, or that rat-bag Artie Shaw. You know he's been sniffing around Ava again.

Sonny (*confused*) Has he?
Geordie How the hell are you?
Sonny I'm good, man, good.
Geordie This calls for a drink. Dolly?

Joan gets them drinks

Sonny Dolly?
Joan Some days I'm Frank's mum, other days…
Nancy She's my mum.
Sonny (*sceptically*) Vera?

Joan appears to be uncomfortable

Nancy (*sarcastically*) Yes. Like one big happy mental family.
Geordie I know why you're here.
Sonny You do?
Geordie Sure I do. You're here for my big comeback.
Sonny I am?
Geordie Sure you are. Knew you'd wanna piece of the action. Couldn't resist the lure of the Sands.
Sonny The old barn looks swell.
Geordie It's a shit hole and you know it. But it'll be great again and you can be in on the ground floor. How about it?
Sonny I don't know, man.
Geordie Just like the old days. We're gonna have those bobby-soxers wetting their knickers ——
Nancy Dad!

Geordie whips the dust sheet off the drum kit

Geordie Let's swing!
Sonny I haven't played in a while.
Geordie Hell, we're all a bit rusty. We just need a drop of oil.
Sonny Comeback huh?
Nancy There is no comeback. It's a figment of his imagination. Dad, you're ill. You're not up to it.
Geordie I'm still breathing, ain't I?
Nancy You can't even keep your trousers on.
Joan Nancy!
Sonny Some things never change!
Geordie If I'm breathing, I'm living. If I'm living, I'm singing. End of.

Act I, Scene 2

The lights change, and we are transported into Geordie's hallucination. Geordie sings part of Frank Sinatra's song "Where or When"

At the end of the song, the lights change back, and we move from hallucination back into reality. Everyone in their original positions

Where you staying?
Sonny Just passing through.
Geordie Stay here. Perfect for rehearsals.
Sonny I don't know, man.
Nancy I knew this would happen.
Geordie Take no notice of (*Singing; to the tune of "Nancy with the Laughing Face"*)"Nancy with the aching face". (*Speaking*) She's just sore because we haven't put her on the bill.
Nancy Don't be ridiculous.
Geordie She's got one hell of a voice, my Nancy. Come on, sing something.
Nancy Oh, sod off Dad!
Geordie Don't you love it when dames talk dirty.
Sonny Just like the old days.
Geordie Highballs and honeys. Where did it all go wrong?
Nancy I hate to spoil the Rat Pack party, but you've got to face facts. This building is a mess, you can't afford to heat or decorate the place. There is going to be no gig!

Nancy exits, having had enough

Geordie Who pissed in her pina colada? She'll come round.
Joan I wouldn't bank on it.
Geordie (*to Joan*) I can't do this without you. You know that?
Joan I know. Me neither.
Geordie (*to Sonny*) What do you say?
Sonny I dunno.
Geordie The old pack, back together, fighting over women and making up over a beautiful modulation and a quart of bourbon. You owe me, kid. Are you in, or are you in?

Sonny thinks about it, then goes to the drums and plays a drum break

That's my boy.

Black-out

SCENE 3

The same

Joan is reading a book

Nancy (*speaking into her Dictaphone*) Fanny pleaded, "Touch me—caress me and you will feel my passion—no—touch me there and—no, stroke my, oh..."

Joan stifles a laugh

Are you laughing at me?
Joan No. Something in here.
Nancy What are you reading?
Joan *A Child Called It*.
Nancy Keep your snide criticisms to yourself.
Joan You could always work in your room.
Nancy The radiator's buggered. Don't know why you want to read that shit. Bloody misery porn. Should be banned.
Joan I've read them all... *The Little Prisoner. Don't Tell Mummy. Broken Wings*.
Nancy More like broken record, they're all the bloody same. Oh, listen to me while I whinge on about how difficult my life's been. All trying to outdo each other on the Richter scale of misery. "Oh, look at my cigarette burns, sorry I can't, someone poured bleach in my eyes".
Joan It makes you feel better about your own life. You could write something about your dad's condition, the reality for family members.
Nancy I don't want to write about dementia, well, not seriously, it's bad enough living with it.
Joan These things sell millions.
Nancy Yeah, well—millions—(*mind ticking over*) Hmmm—I did have it pretty rough I suppose...
Joan You had a happy childhood.
Nancy I'm sure I can drag up some unspeakable trauma.
Joan You can't just make it up.
Nancy Rubbish! Half of those "fiddle and tell" books are made up.
Joan Your dad didn't abuse you.
Nancy After Mum died I was adrift and alone in a frightening world.
Joan He adored you, put you on a pedestal. Sent you to the best schools.
Nancy He never bought me a pony.
Joan That must have been devastating.
Nancy It was. (*Considering*) I just need a pithy title.

Act I, Scene 3

Joan "A Child Called Spoilt Git?"

Nancy's brain is ticking over

The focus should be on your dad. Dementia.
Nancy Yeah, it'll certainly cheer up that ineffectual agent of mine. (*Speaking into her Dictaphone*) Title for mis-lit: Dad's Dementia. He's Demented, I'm demented! My Demented Dad. Dad, Dementia and Me.
Joan Maybe it's not a good idea.
Nancy Shush! I'm trying to work!
Joan I wish I'd never mentioned it.

Nancy snaps her Dictaphone off

Nancy What do you mean? You? It's my idea. Don't try to get a royalty out of me!
Joan You'll need to ask Geordie's permission.
Nancy Legally?
Joan Morally.
Nancy He won't mind. Dad supports me in whatever I do.
Joan That's not the point.
Nancy Don't start preaching, it's so exhausting. (*Into her Dictaphone*) Me, Daddy and Dementia. Chapter One — Where's Mummy? My mother died in an horrific car accident on... Actually, where did —

Sonny and Geordie enter

Geordie is shuffling, very distant. Sonny is clearly troubled about the change in his friend. Joan also appears concerned

Sonny He's not feeling too hot.
Nancy Dad...
Joan (*hushed*) Don't bother him. Settling in all right, Sonny?
Sonny Sure thing.
Joan Room OK?
Sonny I've been in worse.
Nancy Bloody hell! You must have stayed in some right dives.
Sonny This place ain't so bad, must be worth a packet, eh Geordie?

Geordie remains blank, in a world of his own

Joan You can't put a value on a home.

Nancy You bloody can.
Sonny Ever thought of cashing in your chips?
Joan And move where?
Nancy Somewhere smaller, more manageable?
Sonny For his bungalow legs.
Joan He's fine.
Nancy He's far from fine.
Joan Some days it gets him like this, he could be right as rain in half an hour.
Nancy It's rattling around in this place that does it.
Sonny When's he likely to come round?
Joan There's no telling.
Sonny Then how do you plan anything?
Joan We can't. That's why I had to give up my job.
Sonny Were you a performer too?
Joan No, I was a nurse.
Sonny Really? Hmmm, have you kept the uniform?
Nancy Can you stop that please? Dad, I need to check some details with you ——
Geordie Ask your mother.
Nancy I would, but I'd have to dig her up first.
Geordie What?
Nancy She's dead.

Geordie looks to Joan for help

Where exactly did the accident happen? I know it was on the Coast Road, but ——
Geordie (*confused*) She's dead?
Nancy Dear God, do we have to go through this again?
Geordie Ava's dead?
Nancy Vera. Mum was called Vera.
Geordie Vera.
Joan I'm sorry, Geordie.
Nancy Don't indulge him. (*To Sonny*) This often happens. I blame Florence Shiteingale. If she didn't let him live in his little fantasy world — well…
Sonny You're a tough cookie.
Geordie (*to Joan*) Ma, Ava's dead.
Nancy Vera!
Geordie (*to Joan*) Vera, my beautiful Vera.
Joan It's OK, love. (*She goes to put a backing track on the CD player*) Why don't we have ourselves a song to cheer us up.

Act I, Scene 4   17

Sonny Great idea.
Nancy Oh yes, Mother's deceased, Father's deranged, let's have a good old knees-up.

Joan sings the first line of "Sunny Side of the Street", encouraging Geordie

   That tomcat's back!

Joan and Sonny sing the next two lines together, then Geordie brightens and joins in. Geordie starts hallucinating, and sings the rest of the song alone. Geordie then starts to get agitated as he comes back to reality. He storms over to Sonny and socks him on the jaw

Geordie Do you take me for a sap, you phony bastard?

Black-out

Scene 4

The same

Sonny slugs down a bourbon as Joan holds a bag of frozen peas to his head. Her bosom is very close to his face. Sonny is lapping up the attention

Joan I don't know what got into him. He's not usually violent.
Sonny Being knocked out has its perks.
Joan Some people with dementia can get aggressive, you know, frustrated…
Sonny You smell nice.
Joan (*uncomfortably*) Thanks.
Sonny How long have you two been —— ?
Joan Eighteen months.
Sonny Not long then?
Joan Feels like a lot longer.
Sonny (*asking about Geordie's diagnosis*) When was he…?
Joan About two and a half year ago.
Sonny Geordie's the last person I would have expected to turn out like this. He's always been sharp as a razor.
Joan Doesn't matter if you were a brain surgeon or a bin man. It'll get you just the same.

Sonny That's sad.
Joan That's life.

Sonny sings part of the first line from the Frank Sinatra song "That's Life". Sonny and Joan share a laugh

Sonny So you got together when he was ill? Typical Geordie. He gets laid up and gets laid by a nurse.
Joan It wasn't quite like that.
Sonny What a fairy story. (*Jokily*) Unless you're just after his money! This place must be worth a few bob.
Joan Money isn't everything.

Sonny laughs

What?
Sonny A woman once said that exact same thing to me, stood in this very room.
Joan Really?

Sonny nods

Sonny I didn't believe it back then.
Joan And now?
Sonny Turns out she may have been right.

Joan and Sonny have a moment

Sonny Do the pictures of Vera not bother you? It's like she's haunting the place.
Joan She was a big part of his life. He idolised her.
Sonny She weren't no Virgin Mary! A great lass, don't get me wrong, a force of nature. A real tornado. He worshipped her, but it wasn't quite the perfect relationship that Nancy wants to believe. But I'm sure you know that...
Joan I'd better go and see how he is.
Sonny Sure. Tell him, no hard feelings.

Sonny waits until Joan's out of sight, then starts rummaging through Nancy's bag and finds her purse. Joan pops back unexpectedly

Joan I forgot the —— (*seeing what Sonny's up to*) —what the...?
Sonny I was just ——
Joan Just what?

Act I, Scene 4   19

Sonny It's not what it looks like. I am many things, but I'm not a thief.
Joan Then what were you doing with Nancy's purse?

Pause

Sonny Looking for her driving licence.
Joan Her driving licence? What the hell for?
Sonny I need her permission, her signature...
Joan For what?
Sonny A DNA test.
Joan What?
Sonny There's a good chance that I'm her dad.
Joan No. You can't be.
Sonny I think I oughta know. Me and Vera...
Joan Liar!
Sonny You'd know all about that.
Joan Don't go shifting the blame.
Sonny I'm not.
Joan You are not Nancy's dad.
Sonny I might be, I might not. But one thing I am certain about is that you are her mother. Aren't you, Vera?
Joan What?
Sonny You had me fooled for about five seconds. Dyed your hair, piled on the pounds, had a personality transplant. But I can still smell a rat.

Sonny sniffs the air. Joan reels, unsure how she should react

  L'air du Temps. Your perfume gave you away. No point in lying.

Silence

Joan I wear it for Geordie.
Sonny Never thought I'd smell it again.
Joan What the fuck are you doing back here, Sonny?
Sonny That's more like the old Vera.

Joan bites her tongue

  What the fuck are *you* doing here?
Joan I'm here to look after my husband.
Sonny Pull the other one, it plays "My Ding-A-Ling".
Joan You might still be up to your old scheming tricks, but I've—changed.
Sonny So have I.

Joan looks disbelievingly at Sonny

I came to see the kid.
Joan The kid. She's practically middle-aged.
Sonny Does she know who you are?
Joan God no. And don't you dare tell her.
Sonny Why not?
Joan Because she'll never be able to keep it from her dad.
Sonny Geordie doesn't know?
Joan Course he doesn't. And he must never find out. If you're here to rake up the past you can forget it. We've been muddling along quite happily.
Sonny This is wrong. You should come clean.
Joan He's confused enough. If I tell him I'm Vera it'll only distress him.
Sonny So it's best to deceive him?
Joan If it keeps him happy, contented—yes.
Sonny This isn't right.
Joan What do we know about right and wrong? We broke his heart, remember?
Sonny So this is some sort of penance?
Joan He needs looking after. I've seen where this disease leads and it's not a pretty place. He'll need someone to hold his hand.
Sonny You really do love him?
Joan I guess I must.
Sonny Then why lie?
Joan He needs me, Sonny. Needs someone he can depend on, someone who won't walk out when the going gets tough. And that someone isn't Vera.

Nancy enters with some files, unnoticed by Joan and Sonny

Sonny What about Nancy? The poor girl thinks her mother died in a car crash. Geordie lied to her.
Joan He loved her. All these years.
Sonny By killing off her own mother?
Joan Don't be melodramatic.
Sonny She has a right to know. I could be her dad.

Nancy drops the files. Joan and Sonny turn at the noise and see her. Their faces say "Shit! How much did she hear?"

Black-out

Scene 5

Sands Hotel cabaret bar, Las Vegas

Geordie is hallucinating

The Pianist plays the Frank Sinatra song "All The Way". Geordie joins in, singing as Frank Sinatra

Geordie (*as Frank Sinatra, talking to the Pianist as he continues to play*) Hey Buddy, you ever been in love? So bad it hurts? That you can't think of anyone, anything else?

The Pianist shakes his head

You never lived. I'd do anything for that dame, hitch a ride to the other side of the world if she asked me. But she won't. She's the only broad who ever made me feel this way. I don't know if I'm in New Jersey or Newcastle. I'd give up everything for her—well, apart from the music... That's a given. I'd be nothing without my music, a nobody, just some skinny little schmuck from the wrong side of town. But when I sing—I live the song. I am the song. I'm honest. Alive. (*He sings the last two lines of the Frank Sinatra song "All The Way"*)

Black-out

Scene 6

Sands Hotel cabaret bar, Whitley Bay

Nancy (*stunned*) You're lying.
Joan (*with a pleading look to Sonny*) 'Course he is.
Nancy You, my father? There's more chance that she's my bloody mother. You pathetic little man. How dare you come here and—and—fabricate this—nonsense. Are you a hack? Undercover?
Sonny No!
Nancy What's going on here?
Joan Nothing.
Nancy Is the whole thing a set-up? You two looked very cosy, having your little heart to heart.
Joan He started coming out with all this rubbish.
Sonny It's not ——
Nancy What were you going to do, sell the story?
Sonny I'm not a reporter.

Joan I said I didn't want Geordie upset. If you were a true friend, you wouldn't be saying this stuff.
Sonny If Vera was here, she'd back me up.
Nancy Whatever little fantasy you've got going on in that head of yours, about you and my mother, just forget it. She wouldn't have given you a second glance. My parents were devoted to each other. Dad was devastated when she died.
Sonny You were three.
Nancy I still remember!
Joan Do you?
Nancy He was heartbroken. It was... (*She stops herself from going there*) When Dad told me—it was the first time I ever saw him cry.
Sonny Sorry to bring it all back.
Nancy What did you mean when you said he killed her off?
Joan He was talking nonsense, weren't you, Sonny?
Nancy Stop answering for him.
Sonny Joan's right. It was the booze talking. I'm sorry, I never meant to disrespect your mother's memory. I shouldn't drink.

Nancy's mobile phone starts ringing in her bag, she answers it

Nancy (*into the phone*) Dad? I'm downstairs, where are you?
Joan Is he OK?
Nancy (*ignoring Joan*) She's here... (*To Joan*) Your phone's switched off.
Joan The battery must have —
Nancy It's OK, I'll be up in a minute.
Joan What's he want?
Nancy His bets putting on.
Joan I'll do it.
Nancy No. I'll do it.
Joan I didn't think you'd want to —
Nancy (*pointedly*) He's my dad, of course I want to.

Nancy exits

Joan (*to Sonny*) Don't go upsetting the applecart.
Sonny She needs to know. I need to know.
Joan Let's get Geordie's comeback gig out of the way. Get him sorted, then we can think about Nancy. Please—it's just a few days.
Sonny Then we can do a DNA?

Joan nods

Act I, Scene 7   23

   You promise?
Joan You'd take Vera's word?
Sonny No, but I'll take Joan's.
Joan I promise.

The Pianist plays a reprise of the Frank Sinatra song "All the Way"

Fade to black

Scene 7

The same

Nancy (*on her mobile phone*) Yes, I'm sure that's the correct date... I can't check the original death certificate, because I can't bloody find it, that's why I'm requesting a copy, you ignoramus! Hello? Hello?

Geordie enters in bare feet and with a slight shuffle. He's a bit distracted, though clearly looking for something

   What are you looking for?
Geordie (*unsure what he's looking for*) Er...
Nancy Keys? Wallet?

Geordie spots his wallet, picks it up and looks inside

   (*Under her breath*) Dead wife?
Geordie Wallet.
Nancy Excellent.
Geordie Where's it gone? There was a hundred quid in here this morning.
Nancy Really?
Geordie Are you calling me a liar?
Nancy Well, it won't be the first time you've got it wrong.
Geordie I'm feeling fine today, I know there was a hundred —
Nancy Dad, I need to talk to you.
Geordie Did you take it? I know you're broke, but you should have asked.
Nancy It's about Mum. I went to the library, looked in the archives —
Geordie Not now.
Nancy There's no record of Mum's accident.
Geordie Accident?
Nancy Research, for my new book.

Geordie There were definitely five twenties…
Nancy Please, talk to me.
Geordie Somebody has taken money out of my wallet.

Joan enters

Nancy Call the cops.
Joan What's wrong?

Nancy ignores Joan

Geordie Someone's taken money out of my wallet and she doesn't believe me.
Joan Are you sure?
Geordie Don't you start.
Joan Did you not give it to Nancy to pay for your bets?
Geordie It's a hundred quid, I'm not The Aga bloody Khan! (*He continues to search*)
Nancy I didn't put the bets on.
Joan Why not?
Nancy The bookie wouldn't accept them.
Joan Why the hell not?
Nancy Because he'd backed horses that ran yesterday.
Joan Yeah.
Nancy Has he done this before?
Joan A few times.
Nancy Thanks for the heads up! I was mortified. They thought I was gaga. But you know what was more embarrassing?
Joan No, but I'm sure you're going to tell me.
Nancy He still couldn't pick a bloody winner!

Joan laughs

It's not funny.
Joan It is, a bit.

Nancy realizes it is, a bit

Geordie I'm going to ask you one more time —
Nancy Dad, I couldn't give a monkey's about your money.
Geordie Never satisfied, always wanting more. (*Getting agitated*) Selfish…
Nancy Wonder who I take after.
Geordie Your mother!

Nancy What you gonna do about it, bump me off?
Joan Why don't we all just calm down.
Geordie What's she on about?
Joan I have no idea.
Geordie What's the sudden interest in your mother?
Joan She wants to write a book, don't you?
Geordie She doesn't need me for that.
Nancy It's about you and Mum, the romance of the century.
Geordie Very nice, but it doesn't explain where that hundred quid went.
Nancy What was she like? Really like?
Geordie Like you. A liar and a cheat.
Nancy Take that back.
Geordie I'll take it back, when you put it back —
Nancy There was no money. It was never there.
Joan Come on, Geordie.
Geordie She's taken it, I know she has.
Nancy I haven't touched your wallet.
Geordie Well if you didn't take it, who did?
Nancy I don't bloody know and I don't care.
Geordie I want my money back!
Nancy I want my dad back!

Geordie is stunned into silence. Pause

Geordie (*broken*) If I knew where he was, I'd tell you.

Geordie's on the verge of tears. His Parkinsonisms are starting to resurface. Nancy notices his shaking hand. He puts his hand in his pockets to try and hide the tremor, and finds his socks. That's what he was looking for

Sonny (*off*) I'm back.
Geordie (*talking about his socks*) These are what I was —
Joan It's probably time for his medication.

Joan exits as Sonny enters carrying a big box

Sonny Let's get the show on the road.
Geordie Sure thing.

Geordie tries unsuccessfully to put his socks on. Nancy stares at him. She's never seen him struggle like this before. Her heart breaks a little

Sonny Here's your change.

Geordie What change?
Sonny You asked me to get some things to tart the place up? For the gig—remember?
Geordie Yeah.
Nancy How much did he give you?
Sonny A ton. Don't worry, I didn't spend it all. Have I done something wrong?
Nancy Where do I start?

Sonny is also shocked at Geordie's inability to put his socks on

Could you piss off please. Go and play the spoons or whatever it is you do, just leave us alone.

Sonny exits. As he goes, he looks on

Nancy starts to help Geordie with his socks

Geordie speak-sings the last two lines of the chorus of the Frank Sinatra song "All The Way"

There we go. Cosy toes.

Geordie kisses Nancy's head — a thank you. Nancy fights back the tears and has to leave before Geordie notices how upset she is

Joan will be back in a minute.

The Pianist starts to play the Frank Sinatra song "All The Way"

Geordie is hallucinating. He sings a little snatch of "All The Way", then starts talking to the Pianist

Geordie (*to the Pianist*) Buddy, I ain't no ding-a-ling. But these hallucinations—boy—they're tripple-trippier than the trippiest thing you've ever tripped out on. They feel real, but at the same time—I know they ain't. I can see you, in three dimensions. Authentic. Substantial. Undeniable. But I know if I just reach out and touch—you'll disappear. (*He reaches out, but stops himself from touching the Pianist*) So I never do. I never do.

Lights cross-fade back to reality

Act I, Scene 7   27

Joan enters with Geordie's medication

Joan Here you go.
Geordie Is Nancy OK? She seemed upset.
Joan She's got a lot going on.
Geordie I'd love to get my hands on that dirty, shagaround husband of hers.
Joan So would she.
Geordie She's not as tough as she makes out.

Pause

Joan Nancy can look after herself, it's you I'm worried about.

Geordie's hand is tremulous

Geordie You and me both.
Joan You're probably tired. You had a restless night.
Geordie Did I?
Joan Kicking and screaming, nearly gave me a black eye.
Geordie I never thought I'd end up like this.
Joan Best not to dwell on it.
Geordie You don't know the half...
Joan I wish I could make it better.
Geordie You do. (*Pause*) There's a pianist over there...

Joan looks and sees nothing

Damn fine pianist. He's there all the time. He played for Frank for over fifty years. On and off. His name's Bill Miller.
Joan That's nice. (*Humouring Geordie*) Hiya, Bill.
Geordie I know you can't see him. I've told him things that—I could never tell you.
Joan You can tell me anything.
Geordie Not about my visions. I'd be too ashamed.
Joan Nothing to be ashamed of.
Geordie Bad thoughts.
Joan You have good ones too.
Geordie Yeah, when they're good, they're the best. But the dark ones, boy, they terrify me. It's like I'm a prisoner in my own head. Solitary confinement. Skin and bones.
Joan I'm here, you need never be alone.
Geordie Sometimes I wish ——

Joan Yeah?
Geordie I wish I was dead.
Joan Geordie.
Geordie Dead and gone. I wanna curl up in a big ball —
Joan Please...
Geordie I feel so out of control.
Joan You don't need to be in control, I'm here, you've got me. I'm in control.
Geordie I don't know where I'd be without you.

They hug as the lights fade and the Pianist plays "All The Way".

Scene 8

Sands Hotel cabaret bar, Las Vegas/Whitley Bay

We're in Geordie's hallucination. Music for the Frank Sinatra song "The Lady From 29 Palms" starts. Geordie joins in, singing. When the song has finished Geordie picks up the phone to talk with Ava whilst looking at Vera's picture on the wall

Geordie (*on the phone*) Ava, baby, don't give me the runaround. You know how much I love you... Goddamn it, I'm gonna marry you... When I get divorced... I'm working on it, honey, I've asked her a million times. Nancy can be a very stubborn broad when she wants to be... I know you're not some dumb bobby-soxer... I'm going crazy in this dive... Who you banging out there, anyway? Come on baby... Give me a break! I can't live without you... I will prove it, I'll kill myself... (*Ava's hung up*) Ava? Ava? (*He slams the phone down*) You fucking son-of-a-bitch... I'm dying here... I love ya, I hate ya, I'll fucking kill ya... (*He loses it and starts trashing the bar, snatching Vera's picture from the wall, he smashes and tears it up. He ends up blubbering, trying to piece it back together*) I love you, baby.

Nancy enters and takes in the devastation

Nancy Dear God. What's happened?
Geordie We had a bust-up.
Nancy With Sonny? Have you been fighting again?
Geordie She's not coming back.
Nancy Who's not coming back?
Geordie Vera?
Nancy I'm not Vera.

Act I, Scene 8

Geordie We had a fight.
Nancy You and Mum? When?
Geordie Ava.
Nancy It's me, Nancy.
Geordie Nancy. I need that divorce.
Nancy Pull yourself together, Dad.
Geordie I'm begging you.
Nancy No more of this nonsense.
Geordie If you don't give me that divorce I swear to God —
Nancy That's enough!
Geordie You've had enough! I wanna be free to marry the woman I love.
Nancy I'm your daughter, Nancy. Ava Gardner doesn't fucking exist. Well — she did, but she's dead.
Geordie Ava's dead?
Nancy For heaven's sake! She died years ago and so did Frank Sinatra. You are not him.
Geordie I'm not?
Nancy No!
Geordie Then who am I?

Pause

Nancy (*tenderly*) You're George Carson, you were married to Vera Carson. She died in a car crash when I was a kid — remember?

Geordie looks very confused

Joan enters

At least that's what you told me, but I don't think that's true, is it?
Joan What's going on?
Nancy He's trashed the place. He shouldn't be left alone.
Joan I had to go to the bank. I can't be with him every minute. Where were you?
Nancy Trying to work. Trying to salvage my career. I'm really stressed out —
Joan You are! Every day is stressful for me. This is normal.
Nancy He's done this before?

Joan nods

You never told me.
Joan You never returned my calls.

Nancy has a pang of guilt

    He was fine when I left. Geordie, it's Joan.
Geordie Joan?
Joan Come on, let's take you upstairs for a rest.
Geordie I don't want a rest, I want Ava.
Joan Ava's away filming.
Geordie When will she be back?
Joan As soon as they've wrapped.
Geordie (*clearly relieved*) She's coming back?
Joan Sure she is. She'll be on the first plane out of Nairobi.
Nancy I'll tidy up for her.
Joan Yeah, thanks.

Joan takes Geordie upstairs to exit, singing "Sunny Side of the Street" to help him make the effort. Geordie cheers up

Nancy watches them as they go. It's clear that she's beginning to appreciate Joan. Nancy starts to tidy up Vera's torn picture. The phone rings, she lets it click through to the answer machine

Estate Agent (*recorded voice*) Hi, this is a message for Joan Wilson, it's Simon from Your Move Estate Agent. If you could give me a —

Nancy races to the phone and picks it up

Nancy Hello Simon... Yes, this is Joan... Different? It must be the elocution lessons. (*Trying to imitate Joan's voice*) How may I help? ... You've finished the valuation on the Sands, have you? ... Wow! That was quick. So, how much is it worth? ... Really, even in the current climate? ... Interested? I guess I must be! ... I'll be back in touch. (*She puts the phone down, her mind whirring*)

Black-out

Scene 9

Sands Hotel cabaret bar, Las Vegas/Whitley Bay

Geordie is hallucinating. Geordie as Frank, and Sonny as Jimmy Van Heusen, both drunk, sing the Frank Sinatra song "That's Life" accompanied by the Pianist. Meanwhile, in reality, we see Joan going through some old suitcases of Vera's stuff

Act I, Scene 9   31

Geordie (*as Frank*) Jimmy Van Heusen. You're like a brother to me.
Sonny (*as Jimmy*) Well, take my advice, don't fool around with guns.
Geordie No gags next time, I'll see it through. Blow my brains out.
Sonny That'll teach her!
Geordie Cash in my chips.
Sonny Save enough for the cab home.
Geordie Blam! All over.
Sonny You, ruin a good suit? Nah. (*To the Pianist*) Say, how much has he had to drink, buddy?

The Pianist shrugs

    Real chatterbox ain't he?
Geordie "I feel sorry for people who don't drink. When they get up in the morning that's as good as they're going to feel all day."
Sonny I didn't know you drank till I met you sober one day.
Geordie What day was that?
Sonny I dunno. Wasn't a boozeday.
Geordie Must have been a leap year.
Sonny No doubt.
Geordie I don't feel so good.
Sonny That means the liquor's working.
Geordie I'm an eighteen carat manic depressive.
Sonny Only eighteen? But you're so shiny!
Geordie I'm beat. She's done me in.
Sonny She's no good for you, Frank.
Geordie I can't live without the goddamn son-of-a-bitch.
Sonny It's Helen of Troy all over again.
Geordie Jupiter and Juno.
Sonny Juniper and vino. That broad's gonna be the death of you.
Geordie What a way to go.
Sonny That good, huh?
Geordie Brother, she could raise the fucking dead.

Lights crossfade to Joan, sorting through suitcases

    Nancy enters, talking into her Dictaphone, making an ostentatious display of dictating

Nancy Dad had accused me of being a liar, a cheat, a thief. But it was me who had been robbed, robbed of my father. And now I was about to be robbed again, by his gold-digging, pension-pilfering paramour.
Joan Excuse me?
Nancy Where've you been all day?

Joan Me and your dad were having a lie down.
Nancy You couldn't have been, there was a terrible commotion coming from…

Joan "conceals" a broad smile

Urrh… no.
Joan What's wrong?
Nancy That is disgusting.
Joan Your dad's always had a healthy libido.
Nancy That's bordering on abuse.
Joan He's my partner.
Nancy He's—he's—got dementia.
Joan It affects his brain, not his cock.
Nancy Is that how you keep him docile? Distracted, while you rip him off.
Joan (*refuting the accusation*) I am not ——
Nancy Simon phoned. You know Simon. Lovely man from the estate agent.
Joan Ah!
Nancy Why don't you have done with it and call Kirsty Allsop. What you trying to do, shag him to death for a cash claw-back?
Joan Don't be ridiculous.
Nancy Sell up, cash in, pack him off to a nursing home and piss off, eh?
Joan Is that what you think of me?
Nancy You've no legal rights, you're not even married.
Joan He gave me power of attorney.
Nancy You what?
Joan He wanted you to do it.
Nancy Well why didn't he ask me?
Joan He tried. But you were too busy hobnobbing in the Groucho to return his calls.
Nancy You're not selling the place.
Joan We've no plans to. We're turning it into a care home.

Nancy looks aghast

Lights crossfade to Sonny and Geordie as the Pianist plays the Frank Sinatra song "The Lady is a Tramp"

Geordie (*as Frank*; *to the Pianist*) You call Ava a tramp and I'll knock you into next week.
Sonny (*as Jimmy*) Cool it, Frank. He's just doing his job.

Act I, Scene 9   33

Geordie She's my tramp.
Sonny You need to snap out of it! Your career's on the skids and you're singing in dives you would have turned down when you were in the Hoboken Four. Ten years ago you had the world on a string. Now, you can't get arrested.
Geordie I'll be back up there. You'll see. I just need to get through this gig, that's all.
Sonny Well don't piss off the pianist!
Geordie I need her in the audience.
Sonny You don't need her. You can do this by yourself. You're the "Chairman of the Board".
Geordie I'm telling you, if she don't show, I'm finished.

Lights crossfade to Nancy and Joan

Nancy There're nursing homes closing down all over the country.
Joan That's because they're badly run. Good care should be their priority, not profit.
Nancy Don't tell the bank manager!
Joan I've done the figures, they stack up.
Nancy C'mon then, what's your USP?
Joan Happiness.
Nancy Have you been at his medication?
Joan I just want your dad to be happy.
Nancy You just want to rip him off.
Joan I don't care about money. If he's happy, I'm happy.
Nancy So there's nothing in it for you?
Joan I get to go back to work, running this place. We have enough money to survive and lots of people get amazing care. People are crying out for decent homes. We'll focus on the person with dementia and tailor the care to suit their needs and personality. Geordie loves to sing. He can be Frank Sinatra every night if he wants to be. The old dears will love it.

Nancy spots her mother's dress and wig in the suitcases. It is the same one as in the photos on the wall

Nancy Are they my mother's clothes?
Joan I suppose... they must be.
Nancy What are you doing with them?
Joan I was just —
Nancy Selling them off too?
Joan Just sorting through a few things. I should have done it a long time ago.

Nancy Get your hands off. Have you no respect? (*She snatches the items Joan is holding*) God knows what Dad sees in you. You're not fit to wipe my mother's shoes.
Joan Vera was no angel.
Nancy But Dad loved her. He's only with you because he's desperate. He'll never marry you, you're not good enough to be his wife.
Joan You're not good enough to be his daughter.

Nancy is stung by the comment

Nancy You know nothing about my dad.
Joan I know what he needs. I know what makes him happy.
Nancy He was happy with my mother.
Joan I can't bring her back.
Nancy (*holding Vera's dress up against herself*) No, but I can.
Joan What?
Nancy I need to know what happened to her. (*She starts to put on her mother's dress*) I'm going to find out what happened to Mum.
Joan Car crash. You know —
Nancy There's no death certificate, nothing in the papers about any accident. She didn't just disappear. I need the truth. I need to know who I am.
Joan What are you planning?
Nancy A resurrection. Everyone says I'm just like my mother. I might not be able to get the truth out of Dad, but I know a woman who can. (*She has the dress on now, she grabs the case and wig, and goes to exit. Before she does so, she stops to fix herself in the mirror*)

Lights crossfade to Sonny and Geordie, glasses charged

Sonny (*as Jimmy*) Here's to the big comeback.
Geordie (*as Frank*) The best is yet to come!
Jimmy You'd better believe it!

Geordie spots Nancy with the suitcase. Music for the Frank Sinatra song "At Long Last Love" starts

Geordie Ava! (*He sings the song "At Long Last Love"*)

At the end of the song Nancy exits

Geordie Ava baby, is that you?

Act I, Scene 9

Recorded speech of Nancy as Ava. "Who'dya think it is, Irving fucking Berlin?"

Black-out

END OF ACT I

ACT II

Scene 1

Sands Hotel cabaret bar, Las Vegas, Whitley Bay

Geordie is hallucinating

Music intro for the Frank Sinatra song "Something's Gotta Give" starts

Nancy (as Ava) appears in unmistakable silhouette at the top of the stairs. She is wearing Vera's dress and wig from the end of Act I

Radio Reporter (*recorded speech*) The stars were all out at the Chinese Theatre tonight for the premier of Gable's latest romp, *Mogambo*. Rock Hudson, Tony Curtis, Debbie Reynolds, Barbara Stanwyck and the female lead of this little jungle tale, Ava Gardner, all graced the red carpet. Miss Gardner denied rumours of a romance with a skinny has-been called something Sinatra but from where I was standing he was all over her like a mink coat.

Lights up on the full glory of Ava's Hollywood glamour as Nancy stands at the top of the stairs. As she descends, Geordie sings verse 1, the chorus, and verse 2 of "Something's Gotta Give".

As they sing, they dance a duel with newspaper headlines:
"Sinatra and Ava Celebrate to the Wee Small Hours"
"Ava – 'I could have danced all night.'"
"Ava Gardner may tie the knot on Saturday"
"Just Married"

Sound of wedding bells

Geordie sings verse 3 of the song

Headline: "For Better or Worse"

Cameras flash. Ava poses

Reporter (*recorded speech*) Hey, Ava, is it true you're giving Sinatra a break 'cause his career is on the skids? He can't sing any more —

Act II, Scene 1   37

what do you see in this guy? He's just a hundred and nineteen pound has-been.
Nancy (*as Ava*) Well, I'll tell you—nineteen pounds is all cock.

Sound of shocked gasps and stifled laughter

Geordie and Nancy sing verse 4 and the chorus of the song

Further headlines:
"Bookies give 6-5 against the marriage lasting"
"Sinatra and Ava boudoir row"
"Sinatra and the starlet"
"Ava denies toreador tryst"

Radio Reporter (*recorded speech*) Hey, Frank, is it true you've both been playing patty cake out of school? Ah, c'mon big shot, just a few words...

We hear sounds of a scuffle

Hey, are you crazy?

Headline: "Sinatra breaks reporter's jaw"

Geordie and Nancy repeat verse 4, and the final chorus of the song

Geordie (*as Frank; delighted*) Ava, baby, you're back.
Nancy (*as Ava; less than delighted*) I sure as hell am.
Geordie I've missed that ass!

Geordie goes for a squeeze, Nancy responds with a little swift swipe away

Nancy Frank baby, you are an ass.
Geordie Come on, honey, I got a hard-on the size of the Hindenburg.
Nancy Well, just keep it in the hangar.
Geordie Playing hard to get, huh?
Nancy You wouldn't have it any other way.
Geordie What's the deal, baby, you screw the bell-boy on the way up?

Nancy slaps Geordie. This turns Geordie on

That's my girl.
Nancy Cool it, Frank.

Geordie Heck honey, we're married, we're no "Strangers in the Night".
Nancy We may be hitched, but we'll do this "My Way". Your turn.
Geordie Sure thing, baby doll, then I'm gonna bang you "From Here to Eternity".
Nancy Plugging your movie before you've shot it?
Geordie Why not?
Nancy Written your Oscar speech yet?
Geordie We can't all be in quality pictures.
Nancy You arrogant son-of-a-bitch.
Geordie I love you, baby.
Nancy How nice for you.
Geordie And I know you love me.
Nancy That so?
Geordie You came back for my big night. I thought you'd split for good.
Nancy I've got one hell of a thirst, what does a girl have to do to get a drink round here?
Geordie Do I have to spell it out?
Nancy Just pour it out.
Geordie Rye?
Nancy On the rocks.
Geordie A large one?
Nancy So I heard.
Geordie Gee, I've missed you, baby.
Nancy Sure you have.
Geordie I've been real cut up about those headlines.
Nancy You get your fair share.
Geordie Who is this bullfighter bum, anyway?
Nancy For a man with so many hits, you sure do play a lot of the same damn record.
Geordie I'll hit that paella-munching creep if get my hands on him. If you're playing games with me —
Nancy That's rich, coming from the man who pretended to blow his own brains out.
Geordie That was just a gag. A stunt.
Nancy Some stunt. Shame you're such a lousy shot!
Geordie You're on fire tonight, baby.
Nancy I was nearly dropped by the studio because of you.
Geordie I gave up my wife and kids because of you.
Nancy / **Geordie** (*together*) And this is how you repay me!
Nancy So this is you getting even?
Geordie I don't get even, I get mad.
Nancy You just don't like losin' face.
Geordie Don't knock it. This face is my fortune. You're not the only one. Only I got a voice too. The voice.

Act II, Scene 2   39

Nancy Is that what tonight's all about? The big comeback?
Geordie You'd better believe it. Top billing in Vegas, headlining in New York – Madison Square Garden!
Nancy Save me a seat and I'll try to make it.
Geordie You'll be there.
Nancy I don't take orders. I'm not a waitress.
Geordie You're my wife.
Nancy Not for long.
Geordie (*laughing*) What you gonna do, walk out on me?
Nancy You've got one hell of an ego.
Geordie You and me both.
Nancy Fire and ice.
Geordie Molasses and moonshine.
Nancy Why do we always fight?
Geordie Because the making up's so good.
Nancy Yeah. The making up's always good.

They nearly have a little moment

   But not this time, Frank.
Geordie I want you. Tell me you want me.
Nancy I want—a divorce.
Geordie (*momentarily taken aback*; *laughing*) You nearly suckered me there. C'mere.

Geordie attempts to kiss Nancy passionately. On touching her, the hallucination starts to break. The lights flicker

Joan (*off*) Geordie! Geordie! Where are you?
Geordie (*trying hard to block out reality*) I should never have touched you... Ava, don't—don't go.

Music for the Frank Sinatra song "It's Only a Paper Moon" starts

Geordie (as Frank) sings "It's Only a Paper Moon". He's trying to hold on to his hallucination, as Nancy dances and poses as Ava

SCENE 2

Sands Hotel cabaret bar, Whitley Bay

We are in "reality", but Geordie is still in his hallucination and acting as Frank

Joan bursts into the room, dressed up in 70's glam

Nancy (*as herself*) Get off!
Joan What the hell's going on?
Nancy Trust me, you don't want to know.
Geordie (*aside; as Frank, to "Ava"*) Better cool it while Ma's here.
Nancy Yes, let's.
Joan Nancy?
Nancy (*in a low voice*) I dressed up as my mum, to try and get to the bottom of this whole sorry mess and he launched himself at me, thinks I'm Ava bloody Gardner.

During the following exchange, Geordie tries unsuccessfully to fasten his bow tie

Joan I knew it was a stupid idea.
Nancy Well you're not helping. Dressed like a cross between Old Mother Riley and Demis bloody Roussos.
Joan It's seventies chic.
Nancy It might be seventies, but it's certainly not chic.
Joan It's for the show tonight.
Nancy How many times, there is no show.
Joan I've invited a couple of the neighbours, someone from the health authority and the bank manager.
Nancy What the hell for?
Joan He likes the business plan. It'll give him a flavour of what the home might be like, when we're up and running.
Nancy He's humouring you.
Joan That's where you're wrong, he's looking for a home for his mother. You just need to change your attitude.
Nancy Look at the state of the place, it hasn't had a lick of paint for thirty years.
Joan Good homes are about quality care. He'll have to use his imagination for the rest.
Nancy You honestly think he'll want to put his little old mum in this— this nut house...
Joan Says the woman dressed as Ava Gardner!
Nancy I'm Vera!
Joan Your dead mother? If you screw up my plans for The Sands, I swear to God...
Nancy Right, OK—let's humour each other here. I'll help you with your little pitch to the bank manager. If you go along with my —
Joan Charade?

Act II, Scene 2   41

Nancy Experiment.
Joan No way.
Nancy You're always saying that we shouldn't contradict Dad when he's confused.

Joan looks at Geordie, who is getting frustrated and upset with the bow tie

Joan This is wrong.
Nancy It's no different to you playing along with his hallucinations.
Joan Course it is. It's unethical.
Nancy He won't even know it's happening. Just let me have one last try.

Joan looks unsure

Nancy If Dad wants to talk about stuff, we've no right to stop him.
Joan What if he starts talking and gets distressed?
Nancy Then we'll stop.
Joan And you promise to play nice with the bank manager?
Nancy I'll have him eating off my lap.
Joan We're not doing a buffet.
Nancy Shall we do this thing?
Joan If Geordie starts to get upset, the deal's off.
Nancy Agreed.
Geordie Look at that. My two bestest broads. Ma, meet Ava ——
Nancy Oh God!
Geordie Isn't she something else?
Joan She sure is. Come here, let me fix that. (*She starts to do Geordie's bow tie*) This shirt's got lipstick on.
Geordie The dames can't keep offa me, Ma.
Joan Sure they can't, you're a good-looking boy.
Geordie Ava's got kinda sore about it.
Joan Don't you worry about Ava, I'll put her straight.
Geordie You're a diamond, Ma. I dunno what I'd do without you.
Joan (*enjoying the moment*) Me neither.
Geordie (*as Frank*) You sticking around for the show?
Joan Wouldn't miss it for the world. Why don't you go up and put a clean shirt on? There's one in the closet.
Geordie (*as himself*) OK, Ma. (*He gives Joan a peck on the cheek, slaps Nancy's arse and heads upstairs*)
Nancy Hey!
Geordie Don't leave town.

Sonny enters

Geordie Hey Jimmy, you made it!
Sonny (*playing along*) Oh yeah, couldn't miss your big night.
Geordie Ma! I'd like to introduce you to an old pal of mine. Jimmy Van Heusen.
Nancy Does he have to be here?
Joan We need music.
Nancy He's a drummer, not Count Basie!
Joan The local vicar's a jazz nut, he's going to play piano.
Nancy Brilliant!
Geordie Things seem kinda tense? Is everything OK?
Joan
Nancy } (*together*) Everything's fine.
Sonny

Geordie starts to hallucinate. The Pianist plays the Frank Sinatra song "Blue Skies"

Geordie sings the verse of "Blue Skies". Joan, Nancy and Sonny join in with a dance routine

Black-out

Scene 3

Sands Hotel cabaret bar, Whitley Bay/Las Vegas

Joan is busying herself with last minute preparations for the gig and sprucing up the bar

Sonny Is that Vera's dress?
Joan Oi, you, no trouble, we agreed, you're here to play.
Nancy Just stick to the song sheet and don't mess up the plan.
Sonny (*a littled perplexed*) What plan?
Joan The gig's the thing. A smooth show.
Nancy Is that all you care about?
Joan I care about Geordie. (*She thrusts a piece of paper into Nancy's hand*) Tonight's schedule. (*She thrusts another piece of paper into Sonny's hand*) Your set list. If Geordie goes off track, just go with him.
Sonny Course I will, but what's this plan you're on about?
Nancy Dad's not the only one making a comeback. So is my mum.
Sonny Have I missed a meeting?
Nancy In this dress I look just like Mum in that photo. If Dad happens to think I'm Vera and starts to talk, who knows what will come out?

Act II, Scene 3   43

Sonny Has someone slipped her a mickey?
Joan Don't you need to tune your tom-toms?
Sonny This whole thing stinks. Geordie doesn't need this, he's not a well man.
Nancy Dad's only going to get worse, time's running out. I need to know what happened to my mum. I want the truth.
Sonny Then ask me.
Nancy What?
Sonny Ask me.
Joan Let sleeping dogs lie.
Nancy You know what happened to my mother?

Sonny nods. Pause

Sonny Some of it.
Nancy When you said Dad killed my mum, you meant it didn't you?
Sonny Yes. No.
Joan No!
Nancy Let him speak.
Sonny I'm to blame.
Nancy You—killed her?
Sonny No!
Nancy Then who did?
Sonny No one! No one killed Vera.
Joan Think of Geordie, Sonny.
Sonny She didn't die in a car crash in nineteen seventy-five.
Nancy What? How...?
Sonny She was with me until the hot summer of seventy-six.

Stunned silence from Nancy

Nancy Am I hallucinating? Please tell me I'm hallucinating.
Sonny I didn't mean —
Nancy She's still alive?
Sonny As far as I know. We were playing in a cover band on a military base near Düsseldorf. She took up with a pilot from San Diego. When the rest of the band went to Holland, she stayed put.

Nancy takes a moment to try and get a handle on everything

Nancy You and Mum, lived together?
Sonny Correct. Well—on the road.
Nancy She didn't die in a car crash?

Sonny shakes his head

But Dad told me—he lied.
Sonny I guess so.
Joan I'm sure he had his reasons.
Sonny I had to make amends. I had to come. I had to know for sure. I've no family, nothing.
Joan I think we've learnt enough for one day. Guests will be arriving.
Sonny I tried to find you in London, but the place was all shuttered up. The estate agent let slip that you'd headed back up north. I didn't even know this place was still here. I wanted to tell you in person. Then, it all got complicated.
Nancy She left me! Abandoned.
Joan She loved you.
Nancy Don't you start being nice to me, let's hold on to at least one constant.
Sonny Nancy, there is a chance that I'm your dad.
Nancy (*reeling*) No. You can't be. Does Dad know any of this?
Sonny He knows your mum walked out on him.
Nancy I idolised that woman, wondered what life would have been like if only she'd been alive—and all the while she was kicking her bloody height in Düsseldorf NAAFI! She's still out there somewhere...
Joan Your mother's dead.

Nancy and Sonny's jaws drop

Nancy }
Sonny } (*together*) What?

Joan She died—a year ago. Cancer. They sent word because technically she was still married to Geordie.
Sonny For Christ's sake! Look, Nancy ——
Nancy Drop another bombshell and I'll stab those drumsticks through your heart.
Joan I opened the letter, I didn't want him upset, so I destroyed it.

Sonny is incredulous, but daren't say anything

Nancy Dad knows nothing about this?
Joan No. I'm really sorry Nancy.
Nancy My whole life—was based on—on what Dad told me. "Mummy's gone to heaven, she's living with the angels". (*Pause*) I hope she rots in hell!

Act II, Scene 3   45

Geordie (*off; booming through speakers, singing the first two lines of "Blue Skies"*) Testing, testing, one, two, three.

Geordie enters, microphone in hand

During the following dialogue Geordie slips from being Sinatra, to himself

Geordie Come on buddy, we need to rehearse. This is the big kahunas.
Joan I think we might have to postpone the show.
Geordie But we've got the big guns coming, financiers, A and R men. Capitol, RCA.
Joan Perhaps there's more important things than music.
Geordie You know me better than that, Ma!
Joan You need a rest.
Geordie Plenty of time for rest when I'm dead.
Joan We need a rest.
Geordie (*to Nancy*) Ava, baby, help me out.
Nancy I can't deal with this right now. (*She goes to exit*)
Geordie Don't walk out on me, you son-of-a-bitch.
Nancy Son-of-a-bitch?
Joan He's confused.
Geordie Making a fool of me, sleeping around, lying.
Nancy Well you'd know all about that.
Geordie You're nothing more than a cheap whore.
Nancy Get him to stop.
Geordie Don't get Ma to stick up for you.
Nancy Joan, I mean it.
Joan I told you this was a bad idea.
Geordie Who the fuck's Joan?
Joan Honey...
Geordie She's been boning everyone from Brooklyn to Byker.
Sonny Byker?
Geordie I bet you've been through the whole band.
Joan (*to Nancy*) He thinks you're Vera. You'd better go.
Geordie So you're walking out on me?
Sonny Let her go, Geordie.

Nancy exits

Geordie Arrh Mr Bigshot Vegas with his Big Apple dreams. You're a phony, I know what you been up to, sniffing around—I'm nobody's fool, I know who's President, can count to three in a bed and spell infidelity backwards! Oh yeah, I scored high—I was a mini mental state! (*To the Pianist*) Let's tell 'em, buddy, you were there...

The Pianist nods and starts to play the Frank Sinatra song "One For My Baby (and One More for the Road)"

Sonny Who's he talking to?
Joan Bill Miller. Sinatra's pianist.
Sonny Maybe we should call a doctor?
Geordie I don't need no quacks, I've self-medicated all my life—music and liquor. Whatever gets you through the night. And boy did I need getting through the night. (*He sings the first verse of "One For My Baby"*)

In Geordie's hallucination/flashback Nancy enters as Vera, with a coat on, and carrying the suitcase from the end of Act I

Please don't go, Vera.
Vera I can't stay.
Geordie I need you. Nancy needs you.
Vera She's better off without me.
Geordie How do you work that out?
Vera "Not fit to be a mother". Your words.
Geordie We were arguing.
Vera Yeah, well I'm sick of it.
Geordie Let's make up then.
Vera It's not that easy.
Geordie Why's that, what's changed? (*Silence*) Who is it this time? I don't care. I love you.
Vera Don't talk like a tuppenny novel. This isn't about you, it isn't about Nancy—it's about me. I'm doing this for myself.
Geordie You've got responsibilities.
Vera I didn't want a kid in the first place.
Geordie Yeah, well you had her.
Vera I wish I hadn't.
Geordie That's a terrible thing to say.
Vera So I can think it, as long as I don't say it. Right. Great.
Geordie I adore you.
Vera Save it for the kid.
Geordie She's our daughter.
Vera I wasn't cut out to be a parent. It bores me.
Geordie You don't mean that.

Act II, Scene 3   47

Vera She'll be better off. I see the way you look at her, when you think nobody's watching. Like she's the most precious thing in the world to you.
Geordie Of course I feel that way.
Vera I don't.
Geordie Yes you do.
Vera I don't. And as she gets older it'll only get worse.
Geordie You don't know that.
Vera I know me.
Geordie So you're just going to leave her to fend for herself?
Vera She's got you.
Geordie What if I decide to walk?
Vera That's your choice.
Geordie It isn't a choice to love, to care...
Vera Isn't it? (*Pause*) You always said we need to follow our dreams.
Geordie This is my dream.
Vera Well it's not mine. This town's too small. We're heading for The States... New York... Vegas.
Geordie We...?
Vera Me and Sonny. Don't pretend you didn't know.
Geordie Sonny? Not Sonny. I didn't think ——
Vera He's not like the others.
Geordie What's he got that I haven't?
Vera He's young, he's talented, he's ——
Geordie A drummer! I can't believe you're leaving me for a fucking drummer!
Vera He's got ambition.
Geordie I've got ambition ——
Vera You call this ambition?
Geordie It's a start.
Vera It's Whitley Bay! I want to be on the road, see places I've never seen, live life.
Geordie I'll sell up, we'll do it, chase the dream together.
Vera What about Nancy?
Geordie She can come with us.
Vera Being on the road is no life for a kid.
Geordie I need you, Vera. Nancy needs you.

Vera is clearly torn

Geordie sings another verse and the bridge of "One For My Baby"

How long's this been going on?

Vera It doesn't matter.
Geordie Well it does to me... (*The penny drops – Nancy could be Sonny's*) Oh, I get it. Long enough, huh? Wow, you're some piece of work. Leaving me with another man's kid?
Vera She might be yours.
Geordie Might?
Vera I've got to go.
Geordie Are you not even going to say goodbye to the bairn?
Vera It's better this way.
Geordie What'll I tell her?
Vera Tell her the truth. Tell her I died in a car crash. I don't care.
Geordie You should say goodbye.
Vera I can't. Give her a kiss for me.
Geordie I need to know. Is she mine?

Vera remains silent

 Am I Nancy's dad?
Vera That's up to you.

Vera picks up her suitcase and leaves

Geordie sings the last verse of "One For My Baby". At the end of the song he is desperate, he buries his head in his hands

The Lights fade

SCENE 4

Sands Hotel cabaret bar, Whitley Bay

We are in reality. Joan is comforting Geordie, exhausted from his hallucinations. They have all heard enough from Geordie's ramblings to work out what happened the night Vera left. Nancy stares on gob-smacked

Joan Don't upset yourself.
Nancy So it's true. You might not be my —
Joan Leave him be. You can see he's tired!
Nancy All my life, with a man who's possibly not even a relation.
Geordie No.
Nancy Nobody's child.
Joan You've done all right.
Geordie I was protecting you from the truth. Protecting myself —

Act II, Scene 4   49

Sonny You're a good man.
Nancy Shut it, you. You walked out that door knowing I could have been yours.
Sonny I was a stupid kid.
Geordie (*rallying some energy*) You made my life worth living.
Nancy I ruined your life, must have reminded you every day. You gave up everything...
Geordie I wouldn't have had it any other way.
Nancy What about going on the road? Vegas? What about your dreams?
Geordie Dreams are a dime a dozen. It's love that matters.
Nancy Knowing I might not even be your daughter.
Geordie You are my daughter.
Nancy Some daughter! Spoilt brat!
Joan Hey, that's my line!

Nancy gives the tiniest hint of a laugh

Nancy I'm selfish, egotistical...
Joan Narcissistic.
Sonny Hard-boiled.
Geordie Mercenary.
Nancy Alright! Well, that's all in the past.
Geordie Don't change too much, kid. I love you just the way you are.
Nancy I'm gonna be here for you.
Joan We don't want you moving in permanently!
Nancy Thanks!
Geordie *Mi casa es su casa*, babe. But Joan's right, you don't want to be hanging out with a bunch of stiffs.
Sonny Listen to them, Nancy. You don't want to be rotting away in some backwater.
Nancy So I should just run away from my responsibilities—like you?
Sonny I didn't know for certain whether I was your dad or not. I didn't want it to be true, so it wasn't. Then I got to wondering.
Nancy After all these years?
Sonny Lonely years.
Nancy You chose to bury your head in the sand, let somebody else deal with the problem. Well, I hope America was worth it.
Sonny I never made it.
Geordie You never went to the States?
Sonny Nope.
Geordie All these years, I thought...
Sonny Suppose it serves me right.
Geordie Where you been?

Sonny On the road. Scarborough. Hull.
Geordie That's not a very long road.
Sonny It is if you get stuck behind a tractor. I worked the North Sea Ferries an' all, cabaret band. I was at home on those ships, forever on the move.
Joan Different girl in every port!
Geordie So why drop anchor, now?
Sonny I wanted to put the record straight.
Nancy Yeah. Well you're a lifetime too late.
Geordie Hear him out, Pet.
Sonny I had every intention of explaining as soon as I saw you, but then I found out about Geordie, and, well, it sort of sent me into a spin.
Nancy Don't blame Dad.
Sonny I'm not. None of this is his fault
Nancy I'm not interested.
Geordie He could be your real dad—it is possible.
Nancy What if... (*she can't bring herself even to say it to him*)
Geordie It won't make any difference to me.
Sonny (*starting to get the DNA results out of his pocket*) I need to know.
Joan There was a letter. From Vera.

Everyone stops. What now? Joan fetches a letter from under a pile of papers

Joan Her—solicitor forwarded it, after she... I think it might answer some of your questions.

The others are stunned

(*Reading out the letter*) "Hey Kid, If you're reading this, then you probably know the score. I'm a drunk, a tramp, an unfit mother. I'm not going to bullshit you. No point, you can't change the past, but you can change the future."
Nancy (*suddenly snapping to attention*) Hey, isn't that letter addressed to me?
Joan Yes—but——
Nancy That's private mail. Give it here!

Nancy snatches the letter from Joan

What? This, this is a blank sheet of paper! Where's the letter?

Joan appears to be stumped

Act II, Scene 4   51

Geordie There is no letter. Is there, Vera?

Joan shakes her head

Nancy Don't start that again, Dad!
Joan You know?
Geordie I've always known. You may have put on a little around the middle, but you've still got that little wiggle.
Nancy (*taking a while to catch on*) Oh, my God. You're Vera! No! Dear bloody Jesus, God, no!
Joan Sorry sweetheart.
Nancy No! No! No! Is this really happening?
Joan I'm afraid so.
Nancy You knew it was her?
Geordie I played along, why not. She's back. I knew you'd come back.
Nancy Hold on, hold on. Slow down. (*To Joan*) You. Joan, Vera, Dolly, whatever your name is. Explain.
Joan You know most of it. I was wild, liked a drink, liked several. Fell in love, fell out of love, the truth is I didn't know what love was. Not true love. I made my own choices. And I've had to live with the consequences. I know it's no excuse, but I was all over the place. Life with me, would have been no life for you. Me and Sonny would never have never worked out.
Nancy Too similar?

Joan nods

Joan After we split up, I drifted around Europe and ended up in Wolverhampton. I met a man. Tony. Car salesman. Lovely man. I reinvented myself, trained as a nurse. I wanted to start again, clean sheet, be a better person, another person. People don't look kindly on women who walk out on their kids. Fellas hit the highway and nobody bats an eye.
Nancy What about this Tony?
Joan He died five years ago. A job came up in Newcastle, I got an interview and bumped into Geordie. He couldn't get his money into the vending machine.
Geordie She helped me get my Milky Way.
Joan He didn't recognize me. So I thought. I could see he was—but he, you were still Geordie.
Geordie And you were still Vera.
Sonny We've established who the mother is. But who's the daddy?

Sonny gets an envelope out of his pocket and hands it to Nancy

Nancy What's this?
Sonny (*to Joan*) I'm sorry, I went ahead, got a DNA test done. I haven't opened it.
Nancy How?
Sonny Forged your signature. Took some hair from your hairbrush.
Nancy You had no right.
Sonny You deserve the truth.
Joan He's right.

Geordie puts on a brave face, but everyone can see he's nervous. Joan holds his hand

Geordie Read it.

Nancy opens the envelope and reads with a heavy heart

Well?
Nancy What I already knew. Geordie—(*After an impossible pause, a smile breaks across her face*) you're my dad.

They can't quite believe what they're hearing

Geordie What did I tell you?
Joan That's wonderful.

Geordie gives Nancy a huge hug

Sonny (*gutted*) Congratulations.
Nancy This calls for a celebration.
Geordie I'm high on life—who needs booze when you feel like this.

Sonny is bereft. Joan notices and goes to comfort him. Sonny's eyes are on a joyous Nancy and Geordie, as they choose a backing track

Joan You can't win 'em all.
Sonny I was positive… (*He picks up the DNA results and reads*)
Joan We all get it wrong from time to time. Maybe the truth isn't such a bad thing.

Sonny gives a puzzled look to Joan, then to Geordie and Nancy. Slow recognition, Nancy has lied

Sonny Isn't it?

Act II, Scene 5   53

Sonny hands the results to Joan and exits

Joan reads the results — her jaw drops. She looks to Nancy and Geordie, and a smile breaks across her face

Geordie (*to Nancy*) Wouldst thou join me, daughter?
Nancy I'm knocked out that you remember me, Father dear.

Geordie and Nancy sing "Life's a Trippy Thing" as a duet

Scene 5

The same

The Officer enters down the stairs, having caught the end of the song, clapping

Officer That was champion, that. Is there no end to her talent?
Joan They make quite a pair don't they?
Officer The perfect father and daughter.
Joan Who says you can't choose your family?
Officer Sorry?
Joan Nothing.

Nancy approaches Joan and Officer

Officer What a voice. I knew you'd take after your old man.
Nancy Really?
Officer Two plus two.
Joan
Officer } (*together*) Police training.
Officer (*to Nancy*) You don't remember me, do you?
Nancy You do look familiar.
Geordie Yeah he does.
Officer I brought your dad home, before he was famous.

Puzzled looks all round

Joan
Nancy } (*together*) Famous?
Officer Have you not heard? He's had over fifty-thousand hits on YouTube. Type in "Sinatra supermarket strip". Me mam wants to get her photo taken with him.

Joan You said she used to come here in the old days?
Officer Aye.
Joan She ever date musicians?
Officer Yeah. Still goes on about some drummer she used to date.
Geordie Mention any names?
Officer Sonny, something or other...

Raised eyebrows all round

Officer Can I bring her backstage after the show?
Joan We're postponing the show. (*To Geordie*) Probably best, till we let things settle.
Officer There'll be a riot if you try. There's a coach pulling up. Blue rinse brigade. The original bobby-soxers. More on the way.
Nancy There can't be.
Officer I gave out the tickets myself, to my mam's bingo buddies. It took some persuading—but when I said Geordie was on—and that we might have a little game in the interval. (*He waves some bingo tickets*)
Joan But we've lost our drummer.
Officer I can drum. I've always had a natural sense of rhythm.
Nancy Funny that!
Geordie Looks like there's going to be a show after all. Right?

Nancy and Joan share a look and nod their agreement

Joan Right! (*To Officer*) You keep the old girls on the bus for five minutes while we get straight.

Officer exits

Nancy Put your feet up Dad, save your energy for the gig.
Geordie Aye. (*He sits down*)

Nancy motions Joan to one side

Nancy I hope you're not expecting to play Happy Families.
Joan I prefer poker.
Nancy You've certainly got the face for it.
Joan Maybe we could try Bridge?
Nancy If you ever hurt my dad again, you'll be playing Solitaire, get it?
Joan I understand. Your deal. I'm sorry, Nancy.
Nancy I'm not.

Act II, Scene 5

Joan looks unsure as to where this is going

>You gave me the best dad in the whole world. (*She looks over to Geordie*) I adore that man. It's only now that I'm starting to lose him, that I realize how much.

Joan nods

Joan Thanks.
Nancy What for?
Joan For lying about the results.
Nancy It wasn't a lie. That man is my father, he always was and he always will be. DNA or no DNA.

Joan nods. Nancy goes to Geordie

>Ready, Dad?

Geordie Aye.
Nancy Ready—Joan?
Joan As ready as I'll ever be.
Geordie Let's knock 'em dead! (*He tries to get up, but is unsteady on his feet. He sits down again*)
Joan Geordie?
Nancy Are you going to be OK?
Geordie I don't feel too grand.

Nancy and Joan look concerned

>(*Looking round*) Where's Sonny?

Joan I think he had to—split.
Geordie Couldn't face the music eh?
Nancy Good riddance.
Geordie Don't be like that, Nance. It's all in the past.
Joan And we've got to look to the future.
Geordie Cut the crap, you two, I don't have much of a future.
Nancy Dad!
Joan Don't say that.
Geordie The future's overrated, I prefer the present. And this is going to be the best night ever. Everything's gonna be just swell.

Black-out

Scene 6

Sands Hotel cabaret bar, Whitley Bay

Nancy walks into the spotlight

Nancy Ladies and gentlemen—thank you so very, very, much for coming. For once in my life, tonight's not about me. I know, who'da thought? It's about a very special man and his love affair with music and the Sands Hotel. I'm not talking Nevada, I'm talking Whitley Bay, the Vegas of the North-East. I'm talking about a man who had big dreams and a bigger heart.
Geordie (*off; through speakers*) Get on with it, Nance, my bladder can only take so much!
Nancy He's joking. At least I hope he is. Sweet, lovely, caring people, we're going to give this man the treatment he deserves. Please give it up, make some noise, for the "Chairman of the Board", "The Voice", My dad… Geordie Sinatra.

Drum roll

A spotlight picks out Geordie on the side of the stage. He freezes Nancy, concerned, waves him on stage. He starts to shake as he shuffles on. Nancy goes to support him

(*To the musicians*) Change of plan. Skip to the third number.

Music for the Frank Sinatra song "Something Stupid" starts. Nancy sings, encouraging Geordie. Eventually he joins in and gains in confidence. They complete the song as a duet

Geordie I love you too, pet, but get off my stage. I'm fine now. Don't worry, you can sing *These Boots* at my funeral. Until then, I'm gonna live till I die.

Music for the Frank Sinatra song "My Way" starts. Geordie sings the song. Partway through the song, Geordie wets himself. Everyone is horrified and embarrassed for him. Nancy and Joan are not sure what to do for the best

I'm sorry, ladies and gentlemen, I've had a little accident. Let's not beat around the bush, I've pissed meself! Sorry if that embarrasses you, it sure as hell embarrasses me. But, this is my reality, this is

Act II, Scene 6   57

what I have to cope with. Luckily I've got an amazing family. But there's many others out there who haven't, people who need help. So spare a thought for them. Do your bit. I know there's at least one bank manager in the audience, if there's any MPs, councillors, journalists, doctors, come on get your finger out, start caring. Because one day you will be just like me. And we've only got nine rooms at the Sands, you can't all fit in here.

Nancy gets a mop and bucket from behind the bar

Joan Come on Geordie, let's get you cleaned up. (*Into the microphone*) Ladies and gentlemen, I think the show's over.
Geordie It bloody isn't. Nancy, hold the fort, sing *These Boots* if you have to…
Nancy I don't really feel like singing.
Geordie The show must go on.

As Nancy mops, she sings the first verse, chorus and starts the second verse of the Nancy Sinatra song "These Boots Are Made For Walking", remembering the words as she goes, until she is interrupted by Geordie's entrance

Geordie comes back on stage with his tux and underpants on as in the prologue. Joan mouths that she couldn't stop him

Nancy Dad, where're your other trousers?
Geordie Morrisons. Who cares? It's nice to get a bit of fresh air. Arrh sod it, half this lot are doolally anyway, they'll probably never notice. Where were we…? (*He sings the last chorus of "My Way"*) What a knockout crowd.

Geordie motions to Joan and Nancy who join him centre stage

Would you look at that! My two bestest broads in the whole world.
Joan
Nancy } (*together*) What about Ava?
Geordie Ava who? (*He gives a sly wink and cheeky smile*)

They all laugh

Nancy (*to the audience*) Stick around, have a drink. Maybe we'll all get arrested tonight!
Joan (*to the audience*) And if any of you fancy a loving home with a crazy beat for your twilight years, see me after the show.

Geordie "May you live to be a hundred and may the last voice you hear be…" Sinatra's.

Music for the Frank Sinatra song "New York, New York" starts

Geordie and Nancy sing the song "New York, New York"

Black-out

THE END

As the audience exits, Frank and Nancy Sinatra's "Life's A Trippy Thing" plays

FURNITURE AND PROPERTY LIST

Act I, Prologue

Personal: **Geordie:** toupée

Off stage: Shopping basket **(Geordie)**

Act I, Scene 1

On stage: Phone
Geordie Sinatra, Comeback Gig poster
Various framed photos of musicians including ones of young Geordie, Vera and Sonny
Bar *On it*: bottles and glasses. *Around it*: business text books and paperwork
Books stacked around the set: biographies — Frank Sinatra, Ava Gardner and other musicians — misery memoirs etc
Chairs and tables
Drum kit covered with a dust sheet
CD player

Off stage: Tickets **(Geordie)**
Police notebook, *Daily Mail* with the "Nag-Nobbling" headline, £10 note **(Officer)**
Mobile phone, bag. *In it:* pen, purse **(Nancy)**

Act I, Scene 2

Off stage: Dictaphone **(Nancy)**

Act I, Scene 3

Off stage: Dictaphone **(Nancy)**

Act I, Scene 4

Off stage: Bag of frozen peas **(Joan)**
Files **(Nancy)**

Act I, Scene 5

No additional props

Act I, Scene 6

Off stage: Mobile phone (**Nancy**)

Act I, Scene 7

Set: Geordie's wallet

Off stage: Mobile phone (**Nancy**)
                 Socks (**Geordie**)
                 Big box (**Sonny**)
                 Geordie's medication (**Joan**)

Act I, Scene 8

Off stage: Geordie's medication (**Joan**)

Act I, Scene 9

Set: Old suitcases of Vera's stuff, including the dress she is wearing in the photo on the wall and a wig
                 2 full glasses

Off stage: Dictaphone (**Nancy**)

Act II, Scene 1

No additional props

Act II, Scene 2

No additional props

Act II, Scene 3

Off stage: 2 sheets of paper (**Joan**)
                 Microphone (**Geordie**)

Act II, Scene 4

Set: Vera's letter/blank sheet of paper

Off stage: Letter in an envelope **(Sonny)**

Act II, Scene 5

Off stage: Bingo tickets **(Officer)**

Act II, Scene 6

Set: Mop and bucket

LIGHTING PLOT

Practical fitting required: nil
One interior setting

ACT I, Prologue

To open: General interior lighting

Cue 1	**Geordie**: "What the hell…?" *Harsh lights up*	(Page 1)
Cue 2	*Supermarket tannoy announcement: "Security to aisle five."*	(Page 1)
	Black-out	

ACT I, Scene 1

To open: General interior lighting

Cue 3	**Joan**: "You never can tell" *Lights change to Geordie's hallucination*	(Page 7)
Cue 4	**Geordie** finishes singing *Lights change back*	(Page 7)
Cue 5	**Officer**: "Absolutely nothing going on" *Black-out*	(Page 8)

ACT I, Scene 2

To open: General interior lighting

Cue 6	**Geordie**: "I'm singing. End of." *Lights change to Geordie's hallucination*	(Page 13)
Cue 7	**Geordie** finishes singing *Lights change back*	(Page 13)

ACT I, Scene 3

To open: General interior lighting

Cue 8	**Geordie**: "Do you take me for a sap, you phony bastard?" *Black-out*	(Page 17)

ACT I, SCENE 4

To open: General interior lighting

Cue 9	**Nancy** drops some files. Joan and Sonny turn *Black-out*	(Page 21)

ACT I, SCENE 5

To open: Geordie's hallucination lighting

Cue 10	**Geordie** sings the last 2 lines of the song "All The Way" *Black-out*	(Page 21)

ACT I, SCENE 6

To open: General interior lighting

Cue 11	**Pianist** plays a reprise of "All The Way" *Fade to black*	(Page 23)

ACT I, SCENE 7

To open: General interior lighting

Cue 12	**Pianist** plays "All The Way" *Lights cross fade to Geordie's hallucination lighting*	(Page 26)
Cue 13	**Geordie**: "So I never do. I never do." *Lights cross-fade to general interior lighting*	(Page 27)
Cue 14	**Joan and Geordie** hug *Lights fade under music*	(Page 28)

ACT I, SCENE 8

To open: Geordie's hallucination lighting

Cue 15	**Nancy**: "I'll be back in touch" *Black-out*	(Page 31)

ACT I, SCENE 9

To open: Geordie's hallucination lighting

Cue 16	**Frank**: "Brother, she could raise the fucking dead." *Lights cross-fade to general interior lighting*	(Page 32)
Cue 17	**Joan**: "We're turning it into a care home." *Lights cross-fade to Geordie's hallucination lighting*	(Page 33)
Cue 18	**Frank**: "...if she don't show, I'm finished." *Lights cross-fade to general interior lighting*	(Page 33)
Cue 19	**Nancy** stops to fix herself in the mirror *Lights cross-fade to Geordie's hallucination lighting*	(Page 35)
Cue 20	**Ava** (*off*): "...Irving fucking Berlin?" *Black-out*	(Page 35)

ACT II, SCENE 1

To open: Geordie's hallucination lighting

Cue 21	Music starts *Ava appears in silhouette*	(Page 36)
Cue 22	Recorded speech "...all over her like a mink coat." *Lights up on Ava at the top of the stairs*	(Page 36)
Cue 23	**Geordie** and **Nancy** kiss *Lights flicker and cross-fade to general interior lighting*	(Page 39)

ACT II, SCENE 2

To open: General interior lighting

Cue 24	**Joan/Nancy/Sonny** (*together*) "Everything's fine." *Lights cross-fade to Geordie's hallucination lighting*	(Page 42)
Cue 25	**Geordie** finishes his song *Black-out*	(Page 42)

ACT II, SCENE 3

To open: General interior lighting

Cue 26	**Geordie** buries his head in his hands *Lights fade*	(Page 48)

ACT II, Scene 4

To open: General interior lighting

ACT II, Scene 5

To open: General interior lighting

No cues

| *Cue* 27 | **Geordie**: "Everything's gonna be just swell." *Black-out* | (Page 56) |

ACT II, Scene 6

To open: Spotlight

| *Cue* 28 | Drum roll *Spotlight up on Geordie* | (Page 56) |
| *Cue* 29 | **Geordie** and **Nancy** finish the song "New York" *Black-out* | (Page 58) |

EFFECTS PLOT

Cue 1	To open: Recorded Speech. *Compère:* "*Welcome, ladies and gentlemen...*" *followed by canned applause and cheers*	(Page 1)
Cue 2	**Geordie**: "How did all these folk get in my room?" *Canned laughter and clapping. Cameras flash*	(Page 1)
Cue 3	Harsh lights up on **Geordie** *Supermarket tannoy announcement:* "*Security to aisle five.*"	(Page 1)
Cue 4	**Joan**: "No, that's out of the question… I can't…" *Offstage sound of scuffling*	(Page 2)
Cue 5	**Nancy**: "…you might be in there." *Crackled message from Officer's radio*	(Page 7)
Cue 6	**Sonny**: "I shouldn't drink." *Nancy's mobile phone rings*	(Page 22)
Cue 7	**Nancy** starts to tidy Vera's torn picture *The phone rings, and clicks through to the answer machine, as per script*	(Page 30)
Cue 8	**Geordie**: "Ava baby, is that you?" *Recorded speech of Nancy as Ava.* "*Who'dya think it is, Irving fucking Berlin?*"	(Page 35)
Cue 8	**Ava** appears in silhouette *Recorded speech. Radio Reporter:* "*The stars were all out…*"	(Page 36)
Cue 9	"Just Married" news headline *Sound of wedding bells*	(Page 36)
Cue 10	"For Better or Worse" news headline *Cameras flash*	(Page 36)

Cue 11	**Ava:** "...nineteen pounds is all cock" *Sound of shocked gasps and laughter*	(Page 37)
Cue 12	"Ava denies toreador tryst" news headline *Recorded speech. Radio Reporter: "Hey Frank... just a few words..." followed by sounds of a scuffle*	(Page 37)
Cue 13	**Nancy:** "I hope she rots in hell" *Geordie's microphone on*	(Page 45)
Cue 14	**Nancy:** "... and a bigger heart" *Geordie's microphone on*	(Page 56)
Cue 15	**Nancy** "Geordie Sinatra." *Drum roll*	(Page 56)
Cue 16	As the audience leave *"Life's a Trippy Thing" music*	(Page 58)

www.ingramcontent.com/pod-product-compliance
Ingram Content Group UK Ltd.
Pitfield, Milton Keynes, MK11 3LW, UK
UKHW021846210426
5322IPUK00022B/490